Will's Neighborhood

Horace Goodspeed

INFOMAX
COMMON CORE
READERS

Rosen Classroom™

New York

Published in 2013 by The Rosen Publishing Group, Inc.
29 East 21st Street, New York, NY 10010

Copyright © 2013 by The Rosen Publishing Group, Inc.

All rights reserved. No part of this book may be reproduced in any form without permission in writing from the publisher, except by a reviewer.

Book Design: Michael Harmon

Photo Credits: Cover David Scherch/Shutterstock.com; p. 5 Dhoxax/Shutterstock.com; p. 7 Danger Jacobs/Shutterstock.com; p. 9 © iStockphoto.com/thebone; p. 11 Susan Law Cain/Shutterstock.com; p. 13 Junker/Shutterstock.com; p. 15 iofoto/Shutterstock.com.

ISBN: 978-1-4488-8881-8
6-pack ISBN: 978-1-4488-8882-5

Manufactured in the United States of America

CPSIA Compliance Information: Batch #WS12RC: For further information contact Rosen Publishing, New York, New York at 1-800-237-9932.

Word Count: 24

Contents

Will's Neighborhood   4

Words to Know   16

Index   16

This is Will's city.

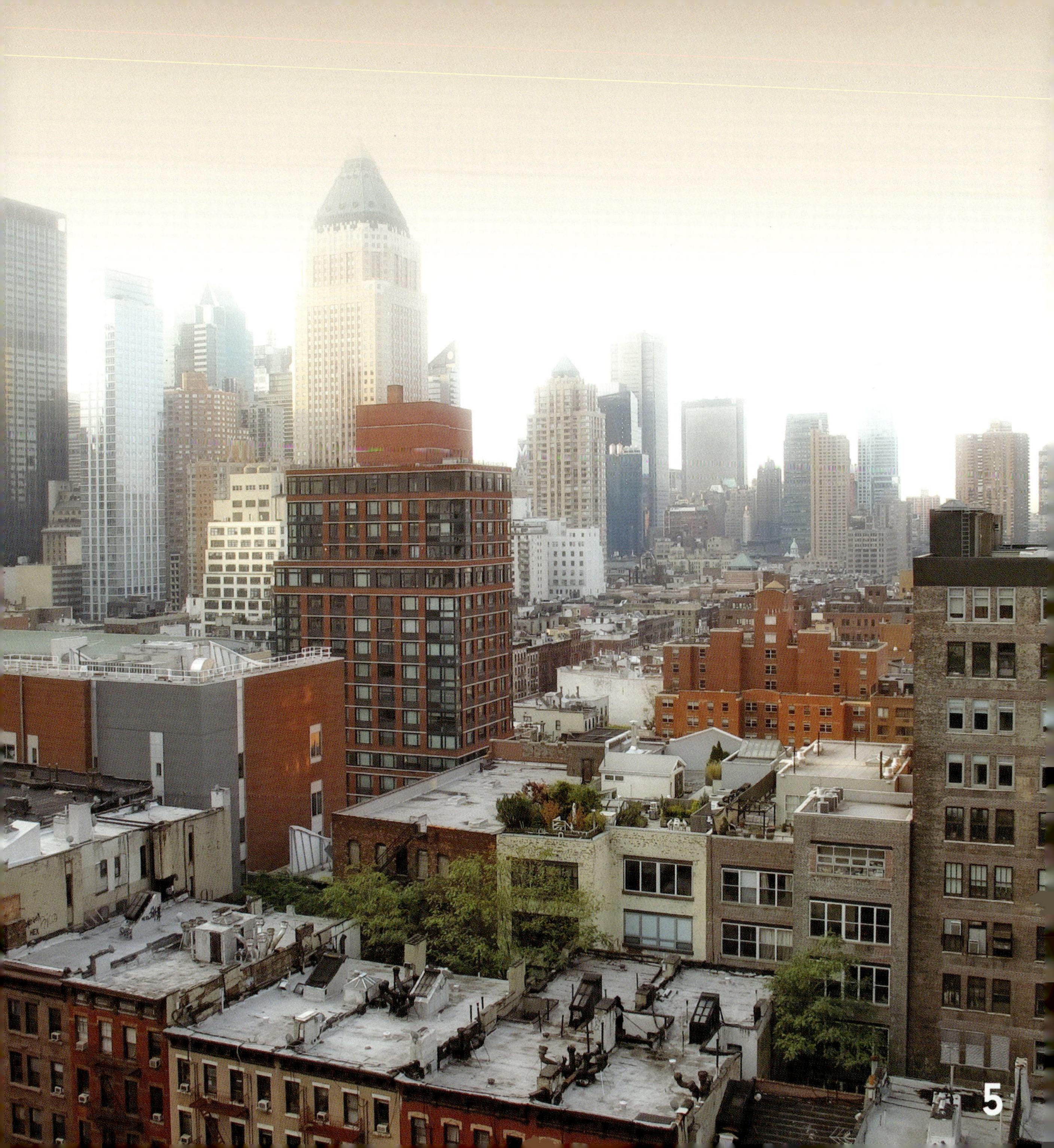

This is Will's street.

7

This is Will's house.

9

This is Will's school.

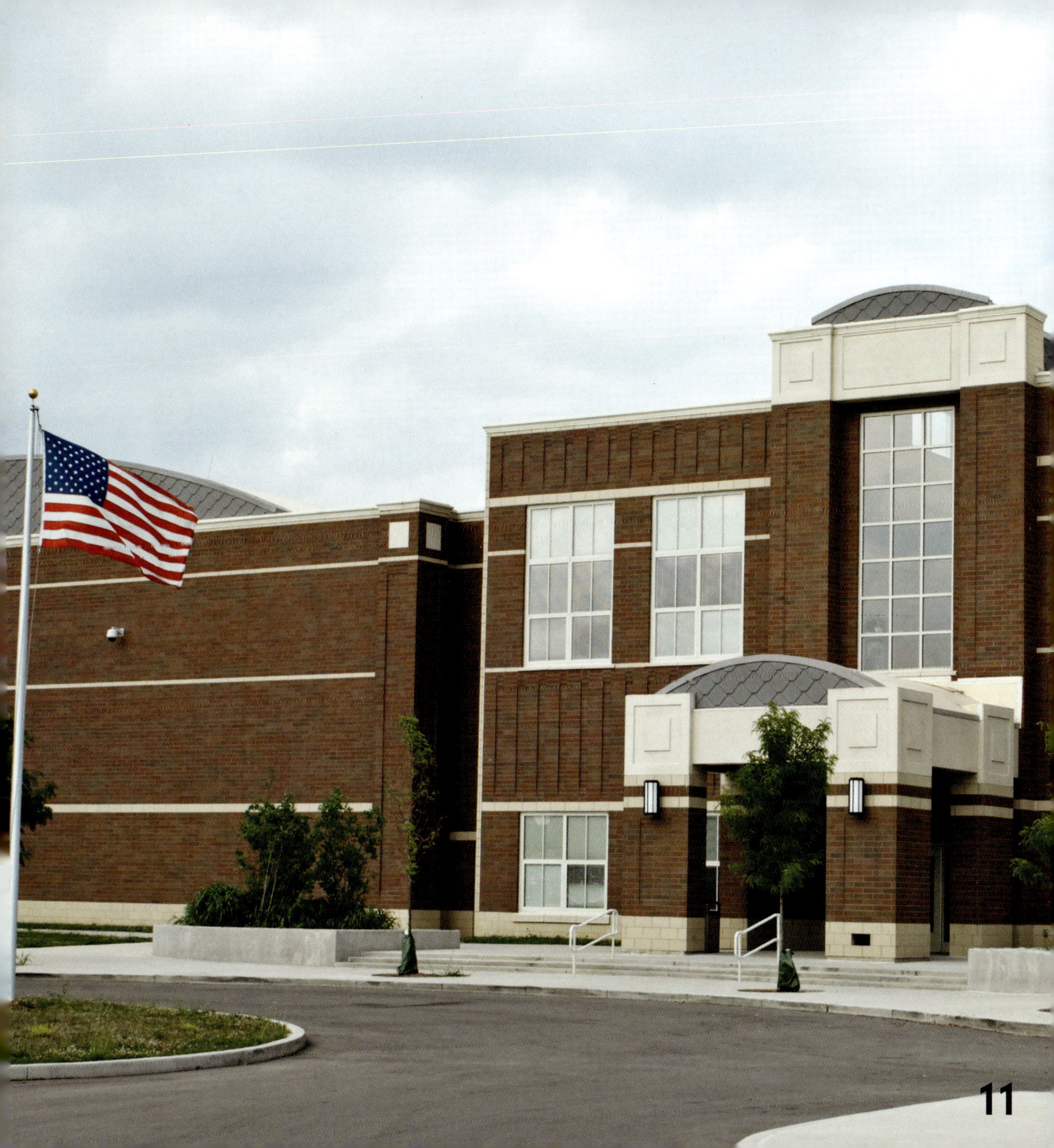

This is Will's park.

This is Will's store.

15

Words to Know

house

park

school

store

street

Index

city, 4

house, 8

park, 12

school, 10

store, 14

street, 6